GOOD ⬩ OLD ⬩ DAYS®

Live It Again™
1947

Dear Friends,

When 1946 became known as the Year of the Wedding, 1947 would naturally become the start of the baby boom in the United States of America. The end of World War II brought love and marriage back to the front burner, and the surge in birth rates that exploded beginning in 1947 didn't begin to decline until the late 1950s.

Families weren't the only things booming as 1947 dawned. World War II was fading from the American psyche, and it seemed that life was returning to normal again. But normal would never be the same again.

The burgeoning economy was on the upswing. And no wonder! There was a housing boom as all those marriages and babies meant the demand for single-family dwellings was huge. The manufacturing sector was growing by leaps and bounds as demand increased for all of the wonders of modern life that new technology was introducing. New jobs, new factories, new homes—the boom seemed to reach everywhere.

But normal would never be the same again.

Education was booming as well. The GI Bill provided a way back to school for the returning men and women of our Armed Forces. Millions took advantage, and the educational ladder of success prepared them to become the teachers, the scientists and the engineers of the next generation.

Yes, almost every aspect of life was exploding, igniting like colorful fireworks on the Fourth of July. In this special yearbook, we have captured those bursts of excitement that colored our lives in those historic days. Return with us in these pages, as we take you back to that booming year of 1947.

Contents

Koroseal coating, developed by B. F. Goodrich Co., was applied to fabric to make it waterproof, odorless, washable and sunproof.

Cellophane Quiz — **HOW FRESH IS A FROZEN STRAWBERRY?**

Answer: YOU *KNOW* WHEN YOU *SEE* IT PROTECTED IN CELLOPHANE

Frozen food producers have found there is more to capturing and retaining the flavor of fresh frozen foods than just the quick freeze process. Part of the secret is in proper packaging. Scientific tests have shown that Du Pont Cellophane is the ideal package for safeguarding the quality and fresh flavor you get in frozen foods. On the journey from freezing plant to your table, Cellophane stands sentry against flavor loss—helps control spoilage and waste in all types of frozen foods.

READY TO COOK CHICKEN

ZERO frost

ZERO frost STRAWBERRIES SLICED • WITH SUGAR

MOISTUREPROOF
Cellophane
A PRODUCT OF DU PONT RESEARCH
SHOWS *what* it PROTECTS

DU PONT
REG. U.S. PAT. OFF.
BETTER THINGS FOR BETTER LIVING
... THROUGH CHEMISTRY

DU PONT Cellophane

Nickel plating on new car bumpers helped prevent rust and kept them looking shiny and new.

DuPont added cellophane to frozen-food packaging to help ensure flavor and prevent spoilage.

Manufacturing Boom

Industries were now fully ramped up and producing goods for peace-time consumers. Many countries were devastated by the war, so the United States became both the leading producer and consumer of goods. The automobile industry was manufacturing new cars at a brisk clip, and the United States was forging more steel than any country in the world. Chemical companies turned war-time discoveries into peace-time inventions to make life easier.

STEEL IS STURDY....STEEL IS MODERN...

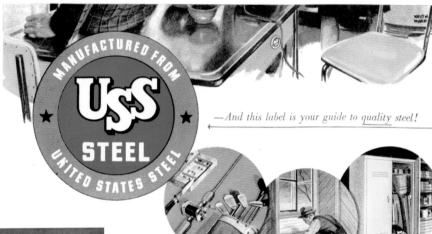

—And this label is your guide to quality steel!

The United States steel industry made products for manufacturing, along with many items for the home.

Imagination makes weather

TO HELP BUILD BETTER CARS FOR YOU

Car companies became more sophisticated, developing automated systems like this "window weather test" to help them test the weather-stripping on car windows.

Cars of 1947

Chrysler's DeSoto

By 1947, car manufacturers began to incorporate features which would evolve into advertised luxuries within the next few years. Items such as gears that shifted hydraulically, safeguard hydraulic brakes and safety rim wheels designed to make tires safer were chief advertising assets for sale.

Cars such as Oldsmobile introduced brighter colors and automatic shifting. Chevrolets boasted of being a low-priced car with big car advantages such as valve-in-head thriftmaster engine, body by Fisher and positive action hydraulic brakes. Some of the luxury cars, such as Cadillac and Mercury, began to lead the way in changing body design. Other features included more rear storage room and comfortable foam cushion seats. Gas mileage was also becoming a strong selling point with some makers boasting engines producing 25 to 30 miles a gallon in moderate highway speed situations.

Oldsmobile Series "98" 4-Door Sedan

Nash "600"

Ford's Lincoln Continental Cabriolet

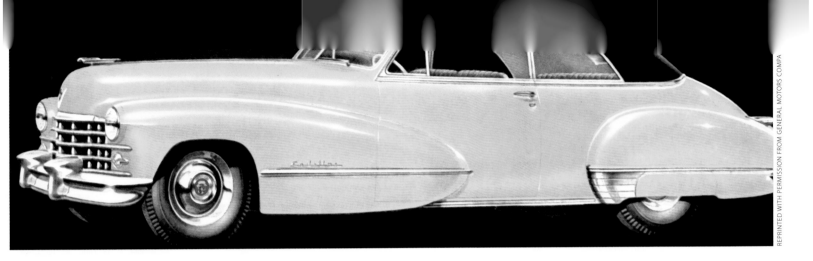

Hudson

Chevrolet

Ford's Mercury

Ford Six

Chrysler

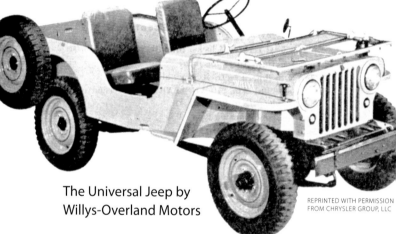

The Universal Jeep by
Willys-Overland Motors

Pontiac's Stream-liner Station Wagon

Frazer

Cars of 1947

Once the automobile industry started marketing American cars again following the war, a theme began to emerge emphasizing a new beginning for the country. Studebaker advertisement keyed in on such terms as "postwar design." Others appealed to new engine qualities such as Buick's fliteweight pistons and Ford's initiation of a six-cylinder engine.

Willys-Overland Motors, famous for making jeeps for the war, now converted its advertising to off-road and industrial use. Riding comfort and plenty of room for storage were also primary factors on designer's minds in the 1947 line.

The automobile industry's reboot included ad campaigns that captured the postwar car buyer's desire for comfort and style after years of rationing and recycling. Kaiser-Frazer, for example, honed in on these yearnings when it stated "the whole world has been waiting five years for just such an exciting beauty of design …"

Dodge

Studebaker Champion Regal De Luxe

Buick's Convertible Sedan

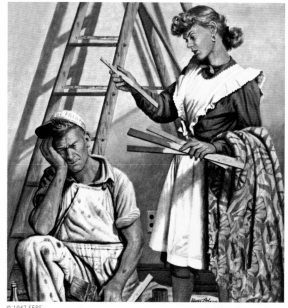

Featured on pages 12 and 13 are Dohanos' 1947 *Post* front covers. He took much time staging scenes to get just the right setup for each painting using a wide variety of models and props.

Artist Tribute

Stevan Dohanos

A July 5, 1947 cover of *The Saturday Evening Post* pictures a son in a World War II uniform waiting on the front porch step for his father who is dressed in World War I attire. The father carries a furled flag under his arm as the two set out to march in a parade. The cover was illustrated by artist Stevan Dohanos, who contributed 123 *Post* covers during his lifetime.

In an age when Americans struggled to reaffirm the country's values in a new world, it was Dohanos' realistic, mostly humorous depictions of objects and locations associated with everyday routines that resonated with readers. Dohanos was, one critic recently wrote, the *Post's* defacto cultural spokesman, whose clarity and optimism manifested the best of American ideals.

Although Dohanos painted energetically during the 1950s and 60s, his 1947 contributions were considered paramount to helping the soul of a nation recapture its heart and culture following the war.

THE SATURDAY EVENING POST

JULY 5, 1947 · 10¢

THIS IS LIFE UNDER FRANCO
By Irving Wallace

TULSA
By Wesley W. Stout

Love Is in the Air

The courtship

In postwar America, couples were getting married at younger ages, and they were dating at younger ages too. It was becoming more common for couples in high school and college to go steady, with boys giving girls their class ring, letterman's sweater or fraternity pin. Going steady also had unwritten rules—no dating other people, the boy must call the girl a certain number of times per week, etc. It also guaranteed the couple a date each weekend.

Movies, dances, sporting events and parties at people's homes were usual "date night" activities. Parent- and school-sponsored activities were also popular in high school and colleges, along with formal dances.

Soda fountains, malt shops and diners were popular places for couples to meet for a casual date.

1947 RECOGNIZED HATTER

Most men wore hats, and it was good manners to tip your hat to a lady. It never hurt to bring along a gift when courting a new girl either!

REPRINTED WITH PERMISSION OF PACIFIC MILLS

Every boy knew he would have to come in to meet the parents and to "pass inspection" before a date with a young lady.

FAMOUS BIRTHDAYS
Jack Hanna, January 2 zoologist
David Bowie, January 8 English rock musician
Paula Deen, January 19 Food Network star

© 1947 SEPS

Formal dances were very popular in both high school and college. Young men and women often worried about the "goodnight kiss."

There was a lover's lane in almost every community and this May 24, 1947 *Post* cover by John Falter is of Falls City, Neb., where Falter grew up. This was a favorite spot for teen couples.

Brides and grooms left the church in a sea of rice, rattling tin cans behind the car.

Any new bride would be thrilled with a diamond engagement ring and a matching band!

Cutting the cake became a special event when the cake designs became larger and more elaborate.

Love Is in the Air

The wedding

During the war, brides often had to borrow dresses or wear suits on their wedding day. With the end of the war, brides began to dream once again about lavish weddings with all the trimmings—big cake, beautiful gowns and more. White satin and tulle became very popular choices for wedding dresses, and silk was available again for expensive gowns. Church weddings, complete with attendants, were what the girls wanted. It was supposed to be a special day to remember— especially for the bride.

Carrying your bride over the threshold marked the beginning of married life.

Love Is in the Air

The newlyweds

Tradition ruled once again—men went off to work, for the most part, and women ruled the roost, staying home to care for the house and the family. Cartoonists and writers liked to portray the newlywed wife as fumbling around in the kitchen, learning to cook and clean.

As postwar manufacturing boomed, couples had many new appliances, new cars and new homes to dream about as they started their new lives together.

"Which room is this, dear?"

Men began to pitch in around the house, once in a while!

Camping out in tents at the University of Wisconsin was an example of the housing shortages on campuses across America.

EOPLE OF MADISON !

VETS IN TENT
EED ROOMS TO RENT

OFFER YOUR SPARE ROOM! GIVE A VET
A CHANCE TO USE THE 'GI' BILL.

CALL UNIV. HOUSING BUREAU
BADGER 580

UNIV. CHAPTER AMERICAN

The Metro Daily News

FINAL EDITION

JANUARY 3, 1947

U.S. CONGRESS
PROCEEDINGS ARE
TELEVISED FOR THE
FIRST TIME

GI Bill

The GI Bill gave returning veterans many opportunities to improve their futures by offering benefits that included mortgages, small-business loans, unemployment insurance, health care, job training and free education. Most famously, the bill paid college tuition, as well as a monthly living allowance for vets in school. This led to severe overcrowding and housing shortages. Veterans also used the education benefits to finish high school or complete vocational, or on-the-job training.

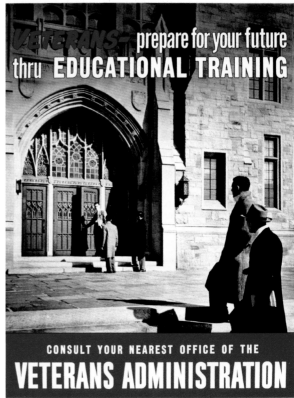

CONSULT YOUR NEAREST OFFICE OF THE
VETERANS ADMINISTRATION

Married veterans with families often had to crowd together in house trailers on overpopulated college campuses.

Veterans accounted for 49 percent of college admissions in 1947. By 1956 (the year that the original GI Bill ended), 7.8 million veterans had taken advantage of an education or job-training program.

Commander in Search of His Kin

DURING the war, some of the professional Army and Navy men—known to the reserves as the Trade-School Boys—regarded the service-academy class ring as a symbol of special kinship and were constantly on the lookout for fellow members of the clan.

A young naval commander, in whom the old-school spirit glowed brightly, once visited an isolated base at which the complement consisted almost exclusively of reserve officers. For two days his inquiries failed to uncover a single brother alumnus of the Naval Academy, not even anybody who seemed to give a hoot about Annapolis. It was very discouraging.

The second evening, though, he spied a distinguished-looking, weathered four-striper at a table in the officers' mess and, on inquiry, learned that he was the SOPA himself—Senior Officer Present Afloat. Observers noted the nostalgic gleam that crept into the young commander's eyes; obviously he was reasoning—and logically—that the SOPA would be a very senior captain and surely a fellow Academician.

Smiling confidently, he made his way to the captain's table. "My name is Dillingham, sir," he announced brightly. "Class of '32. What year are you?"

The SOPA shook hands with the young man and for a moment studied him in silence. Then he said agreeably, "I'm Bradshaw. Of the National City Bank."

—J. C. D.

© 1947 SEPS

Post War Anecdotes

For a period of time after the end of WWII, *The Saturday Evening Post* encouraged servicemen to share stories of the lighter side of their experiences in the military. They called these stories "Post War Anecdotes." Here are a few of our favorites from 1947.

© 1947 SEPS

Said the Air Force to the Infantry

INFANTRY replacements, taught from the start that troops on the move always keep dressed right and covered down, get so after a while that they automatically march as if they're on parade. As the platoon that I was to take overseas covered the last mile to the troop transport, they kept perfect step. In full battle dress—as the newspapers say—and with their packs all rolled just alike and neatly slung, they looked good. The only thing missing was their rifles, which already were stowed in the hold of the ship. We officers, though, were carrying our carbines.

As we hup-hupped out on the dock, we had an interested audience of Air Force replacements who were shipping out too. Their appearance, in keeping with Air Force tradition, was contrastingly informal—varying combinations of uniform, musette bags slung every which way, ranks uneven.

As my weaponless platoon marched smartly by, one of the fly boys showed special interest when he saw me coming along carrying a carbine. When I drew even with him, he stepped toward me.

"What's the matter, lieutenant," he inquired confidentially, "afraid they'll get away?"

—CHARLES A. BIER.

© 1947 SEPS

Parley-Vous American?

THE American soldier never was able to pronounce Rheims as the French do. "*Rance*" is the nearest I can come to it, and that's only an approximation.

One day as we were leaving Compiègne, bound for Rheims, the driver of our vehicle yelled at a gendarme, "Hey! Which road goes to Rheims?"

With a bewildered air, the gendarme muttered, "Reems? Reems?" But when we pointed at Rheims on our map, he exclaimed triumphantly, "*Oho, Rance! Oui, oui. Rance.*" And he indicated the route we should take.

After the close of the war, I was journeying to Paris on a train from Germany. As the French conductor entered my car to announce our approach to Rheims, I pricked up my ears in anticipation of the fascinating pronunciation of the word. The conductor regarded the Yank passengers and suddenly an expression of defeat appeared on his face.

Then, shrugging his shoulders resignedly, he bellowed, "Re-e-e-ems! Re-e-e-ems!"

—J. J. PULLEN.

Soldiers Live and Learn

A POST WAR ANECDOTE

DURING my tour of boot camps our training officer often called on the experienced men to instruct new arrivals in the art of cleaning a rifle, manual of arms, preparation for inspection, and the like.

One day when we fell out with full field packs, he strode through the ranks eying our untidy packs with unmasked displeasure. But finally he came to a "retread" named Donovan whose pack and blanket roll were as neat as a picture.

Walking to the front of the platoon, he ordered, "Private Donovan, front and center. The rest of you men, at ease."

Donovan stepped forward and gave a snappy salute. The captain said, "You have the only neat pack in the platoon. Unroll it and show the others how it's done."

Donovan spread his pack at the officer's feet, but he didn't unroll his blankets.

"That blanket roll is the best part of it, Donovan," lauded the captain. "Let them see how you did it."

The soldier's face turned red and he sighed, "Yes, sir."

He unwound his blanket roll and out of the center of it tumbled a nice, new, shiny stovepipe.

—EX-SGT. RAY ALLEN.

The Puzzling Celebration

A POST WAR ANECDOTE

MOST of us Yanks rather suspected that the British entertained some apprehensions about us while we were training in their country. The rowdies who sometimes engaged in pub brawls, the jeeps which spun spectacularly through traffic, the cowboys who hurled six-by-sixes nonchalantly over narrow roads, must have made life interesting for the home folks—to put it mildly.

The climax of the Yankee menace to the well-ordered British civilization was capped on the Fourth of July in 1945. With V-E Day a thing of the past, we at the Ordnance Ammunition Depot south of Norwich were resolved to celebrate the day in the good old American way. Special Services arranged for ATS, WAAF and civilian girls to be transported to the base for a dance in the mess hall, managed to acquire barrels of mild-and-bitter for free dispensation, and provided almost unlimited access to the ammo dumps for fireworks.

After a very lively afternoon and early evening, the pyrotechnical display began. Rockets, flares, grenades and other explosives boomed and flung fire into the sky, raining sparks all over the landscape and suggesting imminent catastrophe to all. By midnight practically everybody was in varying stages of shell shock from the cosmic uproar. At the height of the mad proceedings I heard a British ATS girl inquire huskily of her Yank companion, "But—but what's it all about, anyway?"

"Why," shouted the soldier through the bedlam, "it's our Independence Day! We're celebrating the day we won our freedom from England!"

The girl considered this information silently. Then she exclaimed, "Crikey, I didn't know we ever had you under control!"

—DAN W. HARRINGTON.

Those Were the Days

A POST WAR ANECDOTE

ONE day in 1942 at the AAF School for Aircraft Mechanics at Gulfport, Miss., great preparations were under way for the "unannounced" visit of a Brigadier General. Barracks were being scrubbed, "G-eyed," mud holes filled, streets wet down, piles of dirt moved from place to place, and permanent cadre men suitably indoctrinated with information on the care and treatment of inspecting officers.

Finally the "unexpected" visitor arrived at the base. He elected to visit the hangars, then still under construction, and to leave the classes until evening. At length he strode into our classroom—an unfinished barracks—and began to converse with the students. He asked several how they were getting along with their work, others how long they had been in the service, and finally approached a fat and perspiring private with the question: "Well, soldier, what were you before you came in the Army?"

The soldier replied, "Happy, sir."

—JOHN D. WALSH.

Mr. President

Harry S. Truman

On March 12, 1947, President Harry S. Truman set a policy stating that the United States would support Greece and Turkey with economic and military aid to prevent their falling under Soviet influence. Known as the Truman Doctrine, the legislation stated that the United States would support free peoples who are resisting attempted takeover by outside pressures. Truman declared that such governments represented a threat to international peace and the national security of the United States. Congress supported the policy by voting to send $400 million, but no military support to the region.

Also in 1947, Truman's administration published "To Secure These Rights," a push designed to end discrimination in federal employment. Truman also affirmed liberal initiatives like housing for the poor and federal assistance for education. He vetoed Republican tax bills that he perceived as favoring the rich and rejected a GOP effort to raise tariffs on imported wool because he deemed it as isolationist.

HARRY S. TRUMAN LIBRARY

President Truman with daughter, Margaret (left) and First Lady Bess Wallace Truman (right) on the back of a train at Union Station in Washington D.C. The threesome was leaving for a visit to Ottawa, Canada, where the President was going to address Canadian lawmakers.

COPYRIGHT UNKNOWN, COURTESY OF HARRY S. TRUMAN LIBRARY

Members of the Truman family gathered at the White House to celebrate Christmas 1947.

HARRY S. TRUMAN LIBRARY

President Truman at his desk in the Oval Office dictating to secretary Rose Conway.

President Truman with congressional leaders (left to right) Congressman Sam Rayburn, Congressman Charles Halleck, Sen. Arthur Vandenberg, President Truman, Congressman Joseph Martin Jr., Sen. Wallace White and Sen. Alben Barkley.

President Truman is shown at attention aboard a ship with Adm. Robert Dennison giving a salute.

More than 2,000 guests attended the royal wedding ceremony of Princess Elizabeth and Philip Mountbatten. The princess' gown was created from ivory duchess satin and decorated with 10,000 white pearls. Her full court train extended 15 feet, topped off by a silk tulle veil secured with a magnificent tiara.

World Events

The term "Cold War" was first used in 1947. It was used to describe the hostilities between the two post-World War II superpowers—the Soviet Union and the United States. The Cold War, and the fears it generated, continued until 1991.

At 11:57 p.m. on Aug. 14, 1947, Pakistan was declared a separate nation from India, and at 12:02 a.m. on Aug. 15, India became an independent nation, no longer subject to British rule.

People throughout Great Britain, her territories and the United States celebrated the marriage of Princess Elizabeth to Philip Mountbatten of Greece on Nov. 20, 1947 at Westminster Abbey.

Soviets show off their military power in a parade into Red Square to celebrate May Day, 1947.

Prime Minister Nehru addresses a meeting of Hindus and Muslims in New Delhi.

News in the United States

On July 8, 1947, the *Roswell Daily Record* in Roswell, N.M., printed headlines stating that a flying saucer had been captured on a ranch in the region. The story went out on the newswires, and soon it was being reported throughout the United States. The incident became known as "The Roswell Incident."

Capt. Charles "Chuck" E. Yeager was truly flying high on Oct. 14, 1947 when he flew his Bell X-1 plane "Glamorous Glennis" at a speed of Mach 1.06 (807.2 mph), officially breaking the sound barrier.

Another "newsmaker" appeared from the skies—the Great Blizzard of 1947. The unusual and unexpected snowstorm swept in from the Atlantic Ocean on Christmas day and paralyzed the United States' Northeast section.

The Roswell Incident revolved around these fragments found in Roswell, N.M., by a farmer.

Standing, left to right: Capt. Charles E. Yeager, Maj. Gus Lundquist and Capt. James Fitzgerald stand next to the Bell X-1 plane "Glamorous Glennis," the plane Yeager flew when he broke the sound barrier.

© GETTY IMAGES

A man makes his way through a snowy Central Park in New York City, where the record-breaking Great Blizzard of 1947 left a recorded 26.4 inches of snow. Seventy-seven deaths were attributed to the storm, which began on Christmas day and struck the Northeast, the mid-Atlantic states and moved on to the Great Plains.

What Made Us Laugh

"My, John, this is fun. Why didn't you teach me before?"

"Well, make up your mind which side you're supposed to stand on."

"Who is she? She comes in late every morning."

"We don't just titter and say 'Well, accidents will happen!' here, Purvis!"

"… and what's more, it's been driven only 200 feet."

"She certainly writes an interesting letter."

"You're fine, thanks, doctor. How am I?"

"Oh, so the backyard's the right width
but not quite the right length, eh?"

Nylon hosiery was hugely popular again when it became widely available after World War II.

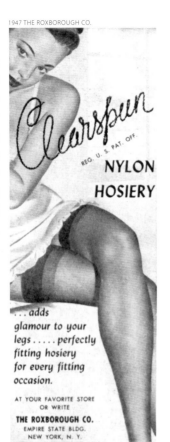

Men took advantage of electric shavers for that clean-shaven look. Women dolled up for the evening in fashionable lingerie.

Looking Good

Prep time

By 1947, industries had ramped back up and were producing everything that consumers could desire, including products to enhance their good looks. Women could buy hosiery in nylon, silk or rayon. Fabric was available for fancy apparel like peignoirs. Men were back in the workforce, so electric razors and hair tonics—whatever it took to look work-ready—were part of their new daily routines.

After World War II, personal care products became a big market.

FAMOUS BIRTHDAYS

Dan Quayle, February 4
  Former Vice President of the United States
Mike Krzyzewski, February 13
  basketball coach
Peter Strauss, February 20 actor

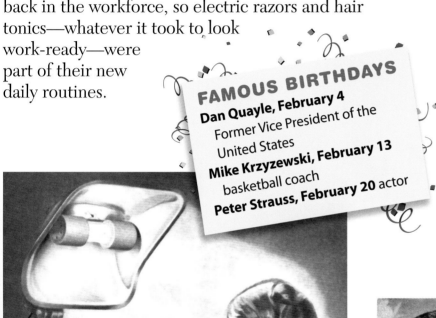

1947 VASELINE HAIR TONIC

Everything from sun lamps to hair tonics was advertised to help people look their best.

Looking Good

Dressed for success

The well-dressed man wore a wide-brimmed hat, usually a fedora, wing-tip shoes and a tailored suit to his white-collar job every day. His personality could shine through with a boldly patterned tie, sometimes hand-painted, or patterned socks. Suits weren't always solid colors; they were available with pin stripes and bold plaid patterns too.

REPRINTED WITH PERMISSION OF NUNN BUSH SHOE CO.

1947 KNOX THE HATTER

Socks were available in argyle, checked and zigzag designs.

1947 WILSON BROTHERS

1947 HOLEPROOF HOSIERY CO.

Suits were cut for a looser fit with wider legs and cuffs. Two-tone shoes looked particularly dapper.

From tailored suits to stretch belts, men looked for a comfortable fit.

1947 PIONEER

1947 THE MANHATTAN SHIRT COMPANY

Fur was considered the ultimate in fashionable, luxurious accessories.

Elaborate entertaining demanded elaborate gowns for the hostess.

Longer coats over suits were a very city-chic look.

Looking Good

Dressed for her best

1947 marked the beginning of "The New Look." Christian Dior introduced his longer, more feminine silhouette, and it changed fashion. Women's clothes became more feminine, more curvaceous with more emphasis on the waistline. Skirts were longer and fuller and shoulders were more rounded and less padded. Ready-to-wear clothing, available at large department stores, copied the high fashion trends of the day.

Men's wear looks, such as pants and tailored trench coats, became part of many women's wardrobes.

© 1947 SEPS

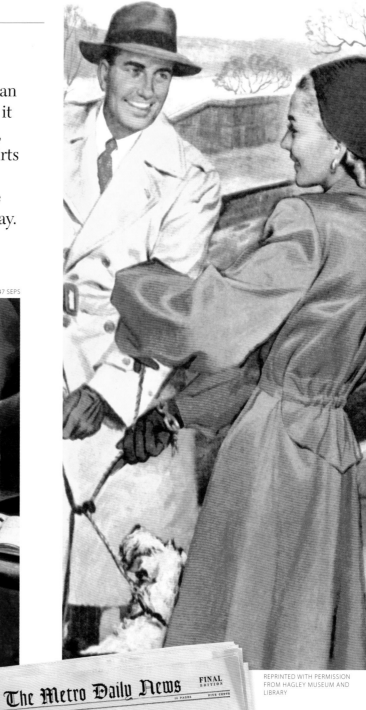

The Metro Daily News

FINAL EDITION

THE WEATHER

VOLUME 17 — No. 161

FIVE CENTS

FEBRUARY 22, 1947

TOM AND JERRY CARTOON *CAT FISHIN'* IS RELEASED

Our Dream Home

Those applying for Levittown homes lined up by the hundreds to fill out paperwork with the hope of being able to secure a home.

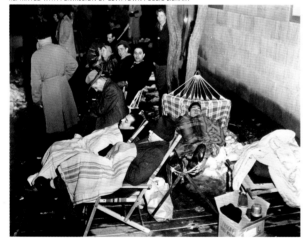

One of the key decisions to ensure more housing for military personnel returning from overseas occurred on May 7, 1947 when the construction firm of Levitt and Sons publicly announced its plan to build 2,000 mass-produced rental homes for veterans at Levittown, New York in a section known as Island Trees. In order to construct their homes cheaper and faster, Levitt and Sons decided to eliminate basements and build their new homes on concrete slabs.

From the moment of the announcement, almost all 2,000 homes were rented immediately, and the Levitts could hardly keep up with the demand. Hundreds of veterans were still applying so the Levitts decided to build an additional 4,000 houses. Within a short time, the rapidly springing community had its own schools, postal delivery, phone service and streetlights.

The beginning of Levittown actually began with the story of the Hempstead Plains, 60,000 acres of flat treeless grasslands that had once been considered the largest prairie in the eastern United States. Over a period of time, the region was divided into territories, one of which became Island Tree.

William Levitt, pictured left of his father Abraham and brother Alfred, was considered by many to be the founder of the concept of modern suburbia through his success in Levittown.

Type 1
"Lookout"

Type 2
"Mariner"

Type 3
"Point Pleasant"

Type 4
"Green Hills"

evelopment plans from Levitt and Sons uggested several different housing styles hich made Levittown a community on hich scores of post-World War II suburban ommunities were based.

As construction continued, Levittown, New York was transformed from an area that started out as an experiment in low-cost housing to an area where mass-produced housing became the most famous suburban development in the world.

Cape Cods

Levittown, New York

1947-1948

FAMOUS BIRTHDAYS
Rob Reiner, March 6 actor, comedian and director
Elton John, March 25 rock singer, pianist and songwriter

The well-appointed kitchen often included a gas range and oven, a refrigerator with a "frozen food locker," white enamel cabinets and linoleum floors.

Master bedrooms often had twin bed sets with matching dressers and vanities.

This thoroughly modern living room had wall-to-wall carpet, furniture with clean lines and pottery lamps with frilly trimmed shades.

Thanks to the GI Bill, more couples than ever before were able to plan ahead, knowing that their dreams of a new home could come true.

At Home
Nineteen, Forty-seventh St.
G. I. Village
U.S.A.

The Metro Daily News

FINAL EDITION

THE WEATHER

FIVE CENTS

MARCH 15, 1947

"HEARTACHES" SUNG BY TED WEEMS IS NO. 1 ON THE SONG CHARTS FOR 12 CONSECUTIVE WEEKS

Our Dream Home

Making it ours

After World War II, more couples were able to buy homes by taking advantage of the mortgages offered by the GI Bill. In addition, postwar prosperity enabled more people to save and dream about being homeowners. Couples had many new appliances and furniture items from which to choose with postwar production in full swing by 1947. Of course, couples still suffered that timeless frustration—waiting and saving up to make their many purchases!

ement playrooms with bars and places and bathrooms with modern ures were on young couples' wish lists.

Our Dream Home

Enjoying modern conveniences

After World War II, steel was widely available, and factories were free to manufacture consumer goods once again. This made 1947 a banner year for new appliances, and advertisers were busy showing off all the innovative merchandise. Women dreamed of modern ranges and refrigerators, and with mass production, they were more affordable than ever before. Small appliances like mixers, toasters, irons and electric roasters were also on most women's wish lists.

1947 KNAPP MONARCH

So many new appliances to dream about—electric ranges, refrigerators with freezer chests, speed mixers, corn poppers and even a "liquidizer," or as we know it, a blender!

1947 FRIGIDAIRE

1947 KNAPP MONARCH CO.

Just ONE streamlined cabinet

Just ONE tireless mechanism

But TWO Washing Units... Switch Them In 1½ Minutes

Thor AUTOMAGIC WASHER

The Thor AutoMagic Washer was unusual because it could be used as a dishwasher and a washing machine just by switching out the washing units … a double luxury.

This canister vac advertised itself as so easy to use that a child could put it together and use it. It was said to speed you through "cellar-to-attic cleaning."

1947 APEX ELECTRIC MANUFACTURING

Women may not have swooned, but they did appreciate conveniences like a new "Sewmachine." It saved time and money, and beat sewing hems by hand!

1947 DOMESTIC SEWING MACHINE CO.

Seeing diapers on the wash line was very common in the 1940s. Women took pride in washing diapers, making sure they were as white as possible. After all, the whole neighborhood could see everyone's wash hanging on the line. Note Barbara Gunn's well-tailored shirt she is wearing, borrowed from her WWII veteran husband.

FAMOUS BIRTHDAYS

John Ratzenberger, April 6 actor
Kareem Abdul-Jabbar, April 16 African-American basketball player
Tommy James, April 29 rock singer and producer

One can only imagine this father, arms full of sporting equipment, thought he was having a baby boy until the nurse announced the birth of his baby daughter. He'll find out a girl can also play sports.

Everyday life

And baby makes three

The return of large numbers of soldiers from war enhanced the potential once again for family life. The result was a postwar increase in babies being born in the United States, as well as Canada, Australia and New Zealand.

By 1947, there had been a dynamic increase in marriages and childbirths. Soldiers who had witnessed the death and destruction of war were experiencing the happiness of looking into the faces of their newborn children. There was an atmosphere of celebration from newlyweds announcing the anticipated birth of children to grandparents and loved ones.

Returning GI's married, pursued higher education and united with their wives in the preparation of new homes for their families. The idea of the American Dream brought a way of life that was simple. Employment opportunities were plentiful as the concept of the baby boomer generation was kicking in. Between the years of 1946 and 1957, an estimated 76 million babies were born. In 1947 the population was rapidly increasing to what it had been prior to the depression and World War II.

1947 EVERSHARP

Filling out the baby book for the first child made the experience of childbirth a reality to new parents.

1947 NORTH STAR WOOLEN MILL

1947 REXALL

Mealtime was often a time for sharing and enjoying family humor and ideas.

Everyday life

Family time

Family time was often a time for togetherness. The evening meal would be a time of sharing experiences of the day. Following chores and homework, family members would often gather to play such games as Old Maid, pick-up sticks and dominoes. Humorous role playing was often a part of the activities with parents and children alike interacting with a personal touch.

Creativity was one key factor in fun, with kitchen utensils, blankets and other household items often used to create battlefields, indoor playgrounds and other play-acting theater settings.

Even homework, grooming for the day and taking care of personal responsibilities was carried out with a sense of teamwork. Family time was designed to include all members in ways that they could contribute and enjoy fun. In many homes at the end of the day, there would be a special bedtime story and prayer.

Reading bedtime stories or sharing special gifts was reserved for times with Mom and Dad.

Children had fun utilizing kitchen utensils and house wares to create attire for play-acting situations. Who would have thought kitchen utensils were just for meal preparation.

The Metro Daily News

FINAL EDITION

APRIL 9, 1947

TORNADOES IN TEXAS, OKLAHOMA AND KANSAS KILL 181 PEOPLE AND INJURE 970

Follow the take-it-easy line

The emergence of pre-packaged mixes such as Pillsbury Pancake Mix made it much easier to prepare a hearty breakfast before work and school.

Canned pork and beans were considered to be a quick and easy food to heat and serve.

Heat...
Eat...
Enjoy

Better get Kraft quality

...good eating
...fine food value
...and Velveeta always melts perfectly

Velveeta pasteurized cheese introduced a quicker way to prepare sandwiches and melt protein into your favorite foods.

Everyday life

The foods we ate

As the pace of life increased and more families became two-parent working households, food that could be opened and served quickly and easily grew in popularity. Americans began to rely on convenient staples such as canned beans and vegetables.

Items such as Velveeta cheese became a protein that could easily be inserted into meals. Ritz crackers were advertised as an accompaniment to many foods such as soup, cheese and snack times. Instant pancake and cake mixes were just making their way into the market. Advertisement characters such as the Jolly Green Giant, of Green Giant Foods, became regular household sales friends to children and adults.

Pre-packed vegetables became more popular with families who were becoming too busy to raise gardens and process their own food.

Nothing awakens the flavor of soup like RITZ!

Ritz crackers became a popular addition to enhance soups and cheese spreads.

On the Move

Family vacations

The experience of a family vacation became an annual event for many wishing to visit loved ones or experience new sites. Growing prosperity and improved transportation means allowed entire families to travel together to places that they had only heard or read about. The anticipation of visiting national parks and places of historical interest enhanced family discussion and preparation for the trip.

Vacations were looked upon as opportunities for education and extended family togetherness. Many individuals packed homemade goodies to use as snacks along the way. Children brought books to read and coloring books to keep themselves occupied during hours of travel. In the evening, families would often play games or join in group activities available at the sites where they were visiting.

1947 NEW YORK CENTRAL SYSTEMS

FAMOUS BIRTHDAYS
Martha Nussbaum, May 6
philosopher
Stephen R. Donaldson, May 13
novelist

Families experienced the mutual enjoyment of such activities as fishing, golfing and hiking. Making the trip back home could be somewhat exhausting to all family members.

Many families enjoyed their first ever travel experience on trains and buses.

1947 THE SUNSHINE STATE

Norman
Rockwell

The postwar trains were designed for comfort, making a trip across the country one to enjoy and remember.

Spacious tables and seats allowed for more socialization and continued business efforts to accommodate passenger needs.

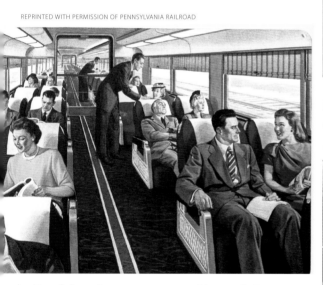

Restful settings were created by reclining padded chairs, fluorescent lights and spacious lounges. Bigger panoramic windows, deeper luggage racks and even air-conditioning were featured to make each travel experience a pleasant one.

On the Move

By train

The train industry quickly caught on to the postwar zest for travel with the creation of traveling comforts to invite family overnight travel. Large windows for viewing, comfortable seats and luxurious dining arrangements were all part of cross-country travel accommodations. Cars provided more spacious rooms and boasted increased speed to ensure quick arrival at destinations. The addition of coffee shops, gift shops and room to roam during travel appealed to both businessmen and families on the go. Excited Americans dressed in style wearing suits, ties and dresses to enhance their modern travel experiences.

1947 NEW YORK CENTRAL SYSTEMS

New streamlined coaches included private rooms and accommodations to satisfy various family needs.

1947 NEW YORK CENTRAL SYSTEMS

1947 THE MILWAUKEE ROAD

1947 GENERAL MOTORS COMPANY, ELECTRO-MOTIVE DIVISION

The Metro Daily News FINAL EDITION

THE WEATHER
City dry Snow—Rain. Snow, Colder.
About 2 Feet expected.

VOLUME 5 — No. 261

MAY 2, 1947

FIVE CENTS

THE MOVIE *MIRACLE ON 34TH STREET*, A CHRISTMASTIME CLASSIC, IS FIRST SHOWN IN THEATERS

Promptness in scheduling allowed business travelers to meet their dates and those visiting loved ones to give accurate times of arrival. On freight, it meant that products would get to their destinations promptly.

In this ad for United Air Lines, stewardesses bid passengers "Welcome Aloft," touting their friendly and complete service from the minute passengers climbed aboard.

On the Move

By plane

After World War II, many airplanes, such as the DC-6 and the Lockheed Constellation, were put into commercial service. Pressurized cabins, on-board lounges and air-conditioning made flying much more comfortable than it had been prior to World War II.

Airline stewardesses also took on a major role, and in 1947, there were 4,077 stewardesses (and stewards) employed by the airlines (up from 1000 in 1941). Stewardesses had to be single, quit when they married and retire at the age of 32. Most stewardesses lasted less than one year on the job, but it was considered a glamorous profession for single women—a great way to see the world.

When Pan American World Airways advertised their overseas flights, they wanted passengers to know that they had English speaking service-representatives abroad to help you feel at home.

United Air Lines said that their meals were created "in United's own kitchens" by Swiss chefs who "added a deft touch of cosmopolitan artistry to the finest meats, fruits and vegetables produced in America."

Larger commercial airlines offered pressurized cabins, "individually adjustable reclining seats and table-served meals," making flying more passenger friendly.

1947 PAN AMERICAN WORLD AIRLINES

Small, private planes like the Beechcraft Bonanza could fly at 172 mph and carry four passengers. Manufacturers advertised the planes as a time-saving way to travel for businessmen.

Flying was still an occasion to dress up, and friendly stewardesses provided complete customer service, treating passengers in a way that made flying seem special.

Fishing became a shared recreation, although the dre[...] of women in two-pieced swimsuits could sometimes be a bit distracting for those intent on reeling in their biggest catch of the day.

An afternoon at the beach with your favorite guy was always a fun way to enjoy a hot summer day. Changes in beach attire were sweeping the country with two-pieced swimsuits and bikinis.

SEAMAN HAROLD DAHL CLAIMS TO HAVE SEEN SIX UFOS NEAR MAURY ISLAND IN PUGET SOUND, WASHINGTON

On the next morning, Dahl reports the first modern so-called "Men in Black" encounter.

Sand and Water

A more casual lifestyle in 1947 led many Americans who had been involved in the rigors of war to the beaches and seas for relaxation. From fishing to enrolling for cruises, hitting the nation's waterways became a popular way to relieve stress and meet new friends.

Beach fashions were revolutionized forever with the development of a two-pieced swimsuit. French designer Jacques Heim, immediately started to work on bikinis. Initially, Heim named his new beach attire, "atome," in honor of the recent discovery of the atom, the smallest particle of matter yet detected. Heim told customers that like the atom, bikinis were now the world's smallest bathing suit.

Other Americans began to venture on to cruise lines or purchase boats for recreation. Still others scheduled week vacations in cottages on the beaches of the oceans or along inland lakes.

Cruises became more popular, especially as the economy continued to prosper and Americans started to look to the sea for vacation relaxation.

SAN FRANCISCO HISTORY CENTER, SAN FRANCISCO PUBLIC LIBRARY

SAN FRANCISCO HISTORY CENTER, SAN FRANCISCO PUBLIC LIBRARY

City Life

San Francisco

Many of the military personnel that returned to San Francisco from the Pacific Theater enjoyed the city so much that they settled into the area. As a result, areas such as the Sunset District flourished with increased population.

In 1947, San Francisco Mayor Roger Lopham attempted to shut down the city's cable car system due to the financial stress that the popular historical transportation system was causing the city budget. However, a public group called "Citizen's Committee to Save the Cable Cars," stirred more of a storm over the matter than the mayor had anticipated. A large number of the city's population of 634,536 fought with inspired energy to preserve the tradition that began in September of 1873 when the Clay Street Hill Railroad began service.

Although tourism ranked at the top of the city's industrial ladder, a banking tradition that was established in the Gold Rush days still played a prominent role in the city's economy.

Rhododendrons in Union Square—the vibrant colors and delightful scents lined walkways that were an urban oasis for pedestrians to stroll or even sit and rest. The square was just one of numerous assets that made San Francisco the great symbol of postwar progress and home for veterans and new families.

The Golden Gate Bridge was built as a civil-engineering project during the Great Depression in 1936 and 1937. It was the largest span bridge in the world at the time of its completion. The bridge was strengthened by two main cables, each which was constructed with 27,572 strands of wire. The bridge connected the Golden Gate Strait between the San Francisco Bay and the Pacific Ocean.

Orchestras and big bands were popular entertainment to accompany dances and formal affairs.

Meeting for lunch at a downtown café brings a smile.

FAMOUS BIRTHDAYS
Meredith Baxter, June 21 actress
Michael Gross, June 21 actor

Ladies dressed in their formal best while attending the opera.

Men enjoyed a game of chess at their favorite club.

City Life

Out on the town

Many of the military personnel returning from the war never returned to the family farms or rural communities. The much larger world view instilled within them during the war led them to large cities for office jobs and the attractiveness of a much broader social life.

Traveling entertainment had become popular. Big bands, well-known singers and theater troops took their show to the roads, appearing in many auditoriums and theaters of larger cities. Movies became much more popular. Family activities would include dinner on the town and viewing of the latest flick. Others enjoyed gathering for more personal interaction at parties and receptions which included more sophisticated games and foods.

Gathering around a piano to sing and enjoy the talent of the local piano player often brought people together.

Rush-hour traffic became one of the downsides of working in a large city. Trying to stay dry while waiting for a cab wasn't always so easy.

"He's waiting to see you—it's about that ad for a neat-appearing young man."

The white-collar executive's well-equipped window office would contain a desk lamp, a fountain pen set and an intercom system.

Underwood typewriters gave secretaries easy-set front margin stops, a time-saving centering scale and "Rhythm Touch" for "typing thrill!"

REPRINTED WITH PERMISSION OF IBM

A secretary who had an IBM electric typewriter would consider herself lucky!

1947 UNDERWOOD CORPORATION

City Life

At the office

While most of America still worked in blue-collar jobs, white-collar jobs were prevalent in cities. Executives were almost exclusively male, and secretaries were almost always women. Innovations in office equipment were making life a bit easier—things like intercom systems saved steps, and improvements in typewriters helped secretaries become faster and more efficient. There were no "casual days," and appropriate office attire was suit and tie for men and dresses or suits for women.

REPRINTED WITH PERMISSION OF CHASE BRASS AND COPPER CO.

Innovations like Western Electric's "Teletalk" intercom systems were time savers for busy executives and their secretaries.

1947 WEBSTER ELECTRIC COMPANY

The Metro Daily News

FINAL EDITION

JULY 10, 1947

ENGLAND'S PRINCESS ELIZABETH ANNOUNCES HER ENGAGEMENT TO LIEUTENANT PHILIP MOUNTBATTEN

The royal wedding took place on Nov. 20, 1947 at the Westminster Abbey in London, England.

What Made Us Laugh

"Miss Leroy! Control yourself!"

"Presents quite a problem, doesn't it, fellas?"

"Ah-h, forget it—forget it!"

"Must they pass so close to the mike? Those sizzling platters are going out over the entire broadcasting system."

"Watch him now. He's beginning to single you out."

"Notice today you don't lean so far back?
I'm wearing elevated shoes."

"It was sure nice of you to let me have
the afternoon off, Mr. Bingham."

"Now, Mr. Hogben, just relax."

Artist John Falter chose the New York Yankee stadium to be the subject for this April 19, 1947 *Post* cover. Research forced John to attend at least three very good games between the Yankees and the Boston Red Sox.

JOHN FALTER

Sporting Champions

Following the interrupted sports schedules of the war years, the full return of professional competition was a morale booster to a nation looking for victories in all areas of life. Jackie Robinson broke the color barrier in professional baseball as the first African-American to play in the majors. Robinson's presence was further enhanced by the opportunity to play on the Brooklyn Dodgers for the World Series.

The New York Yankees continued their dominance of baseball with a winning 4–3 game series capturing the 1947 World Series over the Brooklyn Dodgers. At Yankee Stadium, Babe Ruth, dying of throat cancer, declared that, "the only real game I think in the world is baseball."

The Chicago Cardinals defeated the Philadelphia Eagles, 28–21, to win the National Football League championship. Mauri Rose, originally from Columbus, Ohio, won the Indianapolis 500.

In men's golf, Jimmy Demaret won the Master's Tournament, Lew Worsham captured the U.S. Open and Jim Ferrier claimed the PGA Championship. In women's golf, Babe Zaharias had become popular as the first female golf celebrity.

Mauri Rose, winner of the 1947 Indianapolis 500, received a hug from actress Carole Landis following the race.

The new infield of the Brooklyn Dodgers included the first African-American to play major league baseball. Pictured with Jackie Robinson (right) are Spider Jorgensen, Eddie Stanky and Pee Wee Reese.

Barb Zaharias became the first female golf celebrity. In 1947, she won her second consecutive Women's Amateur Golf Championship and the British Ladies Amateur Golf Championship, the first American to do so.

Sporting Champions

Football and boxing

The National Football League championship was held at Comiskey Park in Chicago and featured the Western Division champion Chicago Cardinals taking on Eastern Division champion Philadelphia Eagles. Both teams were making their first appearance ever in the championship game which was won by the Cardinals, 28–21. The Cardinals later moved to St. Louis and then to Arizona.

Joe Louis and Rocky Graziano dominated the world of boxing. Louis, who developed a reputation as an honest, hard-working fighter, was the world heavyweight boxing champion from 1937 to 1949. Graziano, an outstanding Italian-American middleweight boxer, was considered to be one of the greatest knockout artists in boxing history.

Watching football games became one of America's favorite pastimes.

© 1947 SEPS

THE SATURDAY EVENING

POST

NOVEMBER 1, 1947   10¢

HIGH LIGHTS FROM
GENERAL PATTON'S OWN STORY

The enthusiastic crowd is cheering as the football team makes their appearance before the start of the game. Artist John Falter chose the Princeton stadium for his background of this Nov. 1, 1947 *Post* cover.

Rocky Graziano continued his dominance of middleweight boxing and was ranked 23rd on *Ring Magazine's* list of the greatest punchers of all-time. He became world middleweight champion in July of 1947 when he stopped Tony Zale (right) in six rounds.

Heavyweight boxer Joe Louis maintained world heavyweight championship status for 140 consecutive months. During that time, he participated in 27 championship fights, including a controversial matchup with Jersey Joe Walcott at Madison Square Garden on Dec. 5, 1947, in which he was declared the winner in a split decision.

Dodge advertised this "job rated" truck capable of handling tough jobs in difficult weather situations.

Dodge trucks were built to fit a specific hauling or delivery job.

Trucks such as this one-ton Studebaker pickup were built to be fuel efficient.

In 1947, over 100,000 motor trucks a day were hauling milk to all parts of the country.

Trucks on the Move

The postwar era signaled the opportunity to pour products such as gasoline and oil back into the American economy. Manufacturing companies turned their focus from creating war vehicles to creating durable trucks to facilitate needs of a booming economy. Products such as milk, soft drinks and various foods were transported on a 24-hour basis. Delivery of petroleum products was offered daily to business and residential customers.

Though gas rationing had long ceased to be a factor, increased fuel efficiency, as well as performance and durability were value-oriented benefits manufacturers used in marketing trucks to farmers and businesses. America's expansion efforts required robust vehicles, so advertising copy accentuated that need with words such as "reliability," "precision," and "versatility." White Motor Company delineated itself from the competition by highlighting its capacity to build specialized transports to carry everything from coal to milk.

The prospering transportation industry also meant the creation of more jobs for men who could drive trucks and assist in the delivery of products.

1947 WHITE MOTOR COMPANY

Trucks made by the White Motor Company transported thousands of bottles of beverages each day.

1947 DIAMOND T MOTOR CAR CO.

Diamond T Motor Company built trucks capable of hauling motor oil in all road conditions.

1947 WHITE MOTOR COMPANY

Coal, still a product of widespread versatile use, demanded heavy truck efficiency and strength.

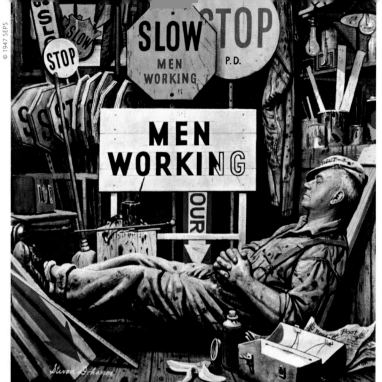

Artist Mead Schaeffer captures a moss harvest distinctive to the South in the bayou area of Louisiana for this April 3, 1947 *Post* cover. Schaeffer said it looked a little like taking down the Christmas decorations. The moss is dried and used in upholstering as filling.

The Metro Daily News

FINAL EDITION

AUGUST 9, 1947

"SMOKE!, SMOKE!, SMOKE! (THAT CIGARETTE)" SUNG BY TEX WILLIAMS IS NO. 1 FOR SIX CONSECUTIVE WEEKS

All in a Day's Work

The labor force which had developed to assist with World War II needs expanded to embrace those returning from the military in the midst of a growing economy. Jobs varied as the number of workers available provided opportunity for income to baby boomer families.

The conversion of the automotive industry from wartime equipment to American vehicles created subsidiary companies that embraced a new growing labor force. Other employers offered new services, such as home delivery, all of which created new employment opportunities.

The rejuvenation of city and county infrastructure created a variety of jobs ranging from sanitation to street construction and repairs.

This Jan. 4, 1947 *Post* cover is Times Square as seen from Herald Square early New Year's morning. Artist Stevan Dohanos sketched himself in the role of the reveler and the New York Department of Sanitation provided the rest of the cast. Dohanos said the job was "the most gracious example of co-operation I ever had."

© 1947 SEPS

Industrial Power

BIG machinery

Research used to develop heavy equipment during the war was utilized in providing equipment for heavy construction, infrastructure installment and road work once the war was over. Equipment used to serve war purposes in rough terrain was converted to installation and heavy work in mountain areas of the United States.

International Harvester advertised heavy equipment that would ease manpower and increase job productivity. International Diesel was promoted as setting the pace for progress in industrial power. With the development of new highway systems and landscaping of subdivisions, needs increased for heavy equipment to break the way for large industry modernization projects.

Pittsburgh is the location of this April 26, 1947 *Post* cover by John Atherton. He found a heap of rusty scrap iron in which the derrick operator planted a small but prosperous garden. The plot wasn't much larger than a small rug, but the crops were doing very well when it was discovered.

ernational Harvester became one of the
ders in creating diesel tractors and engines
set the pace for progress in industrial use.

This Northwestern site is from the Mesabi Range in Northern
Minnesota where the largest deposit of high-grade iron was
discovered. The huge pit dug from this range seemed to awe
the eyes of artist John Atherton as he sketched this *Post* cover
of Nov. 22, 1947. Atherton compared this pit as "bigger than
the Grand Canyon."

GMC trucks that had served heavy equipment
jobs during the war were now being converted
for heavy industrial use in various work projects.

Industrial Power

Building new roads

In 1947, government officials anticipating a rapid increase in national travel, worked with the road construction industry to build up to $1.5 million worth of new construction. The postwar economic boom required a rapid increase in road building to serve newly constructed airports, dams, bridges, schools, churches, homes and businesses emerging in the local community.

Following a four-year lapse in American construction because of World War II needs, building got underway quickly following the end of the war. A large backlog of plans waiting for the return of a peacetime economy demanded road construction and new infrastructure development. A rapid increase in metropolitan population called for answers to accommodate traffic flow and congestion problems.

Road construction workers looked to manufacturers of industrial power equipment to help speed up creation of a safer highway network.

INTERNATIONAL Industrial Power

INTERNATIONAL HARVESTER

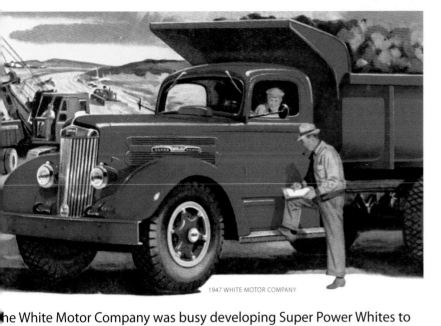

1947 WHITE MOTOR COMPANY

The White Motor Company was busy developing Super Power Whites to help respond to an increasing need for road construction.

Road construction companies were called upon to design and build highway systems to help address the rapid increase of transportation travel, especially in metropolitan areas.

What is America?

STRUCTURES OF A
AIRPORTS
DAMS
BRIDGES
ROADS
HOSPITALS
SCHOOLS
CHURCHES
HOMES

The Allis-Chalmers Model HD-5 2-cycle diesel tractor was designed specifically for heavy equipment use.

ALLIS-CHALMERS
TRACTOR DIVISION • MILWAUKEE 1, U.S.A.

2-CYCLE DIESEL CRAWLER TRACTORS • ROAD MACHINERY
FARM AND INDUSTRIAL WHEEL TRACTORS • FARM EQU

FAMOUS BIRTHDAYS
Colleen Corby, August 3 fashion model
Emiliano Díez, August 26 Cuban actor

Everyday Life

What we did for fun

Going to summer camp was one of the highlights of the year for young people who spent most of their time living in routines at home. Leaving other family members for a week often brought a tear and a moment of doubt, but that all changed once they arrived and made new friendships. On the home front, special activities included attending matinee movies or going to the circus.

Many of the *The Saturday Evening Post* covers have a story to be told of how the artist staged the scene. We've included these behind-the-scenes notes of how Norman Rockwell and Stevan Dohanos created these works of art.

To get just the right setup for this June 21, 1947 *Post* cover, artist Stevan Dohanos spent all day at the Grand Central Station in New York City to observe the departure of children leaving for summer camp. Dohanos discovered when it came time for the train to pull out of the station, some of the children broke into tears when leaving their parents.

Norman Rockwell went all out to create this May 3, 1947 *Post* cover scene. Rockwell contacted King Reid shows and borrowed their wild-woman banner and two of the beautiful merry-go-round horses, lovingly carved in Austria and weighing 365 pounds each. This spirited team was loaded into a truck and hauled to Rockwell's home in Arlington, Vt.

For this Sept. 6, 1947 *Post* cover, artist Stevan Dohanos spent a Saturday attending a marathon matinee enjoyed by many children. He observed lots of the youngsters had bubble gum. The next step was to visit Bedford Elementary School in Dohanos' hometown of Westport, Conn., to photograph a fine set of small children having fun with bubble gum. Dohanos brought along a load of bubble gum to hand out to the children. As he left the school he received a note from a pupil. The note given to Dohanos read "I have an idea for a cover—your neck being wrung by the teachers who will have to fight bubble gum all afternoon." The note was signed by one of the teachers. Bubble gum was strictly prohibited at the school.

Inventing games encouraged creative thinking. It was always fun to play with all the neighbor kids.

What started out as a fishing trip often led to other adventures, such as discovering a dead skunk or finding a new pet.

School books often took a back seat to such activities as fishing with friends.

Pulling clothes out of the closet and utilizng neighborhood pets to put together a circus in the family driveway was always a highlight. Even Mom and Dad got into the act.

Everyday Life

We made our own fun

Children of 1947 developed a sense of creative thinking by inventing their own fun. Neighborhood games would often consist of organizing a local club, playing house or planning shows and circuses. Games such as hide-and-seek, hopscotch or "red rover" were also popular as backyard activities.

Imitating a school setting was always rewarded by taking turns with the role of teacher. Those who had access to a pond or stream enjoyed taking their cane poles for a fishing expedition, although sometimes the catch might be a straw hat or someone's shirt collar.

1947 ELECTRIC LIGHT AND POWER COMPANIES

REPRINTED WITH PERMISSION OF FEDERAL-MOGUL CORPORATION

Tossing clothes on shore and jumping into a pond was always a quick way to refresh on a hot summer afternoon.

REPRINTED WITH PERMISSION FROM
REVERE COPPER PRODUCTS, INC.

Everyday Life

Teen years

The high school years were considered by many to be "the best years of our lives." Due to postwar prosperity, teenagers were increasingly able to finish high school, without the responsibilities of full-time work. Many teens still took on part-time jobs as babysitters, newspaper boys or soda jerks. But, for many, weekends were times to have fun with your friends (or a steady date!) at parties, dances, the movies or the local soda-fountain.

High school students enjoyed going to dances, all dressed up in their finest for the evening.

Barn dances, supervised by adults, offered wholesome fun for teenagers on the weekends.

Girls always enjoyed it when a graduating senior would write something clever, or better yet, a heartfelt sentiment in their year book

Babysitting was a common job for young teenage girls, but it could be a tough way to earn spending money!

A pretty young face was certain to get the most attention from the young guy working behind the counter (much to the other customers' dismay!).

What Made Us Laugh

"Do you have a credit plan?"

"In the book she turns him into a
plum pudding—"

"My glasses are straight; it's my ears that are crooked."

"I like you too, Johnny."

"Since this is washday, suppose we find a new site for today's secret meeting of the 'Little Four,' eh?"

"Our father wants to know if your prices have come down yet!"

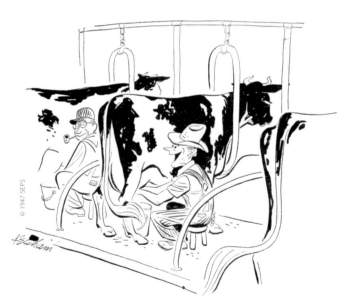

"You're right … it was Yankee Doodle. Now guess this one … ."

"You see how he likes you?"

Butch, the black and white cocker spaniel, was the mischievous star of 25 covers for *The Saturday Evening Post* in the 1940s. He belonged to artist Al Staehle, and he was really a pretty well-behaved little pooch! The four illustrations of Butch on pages 86 and 87 are Staehle's 1947 *Post* covers.

Butch, Cover Dog

Butch made his debut on the cover of *The Saturday Evening Post* on Feb. 19, 1944. He was shown chewing up war rationing stamps, and that cover generated lots of mail, everything from people defending his behavior to actual stamps to replace what he had supposedly destroyed.

Butch and his brand of mischief and mayhem went on to star on 25 *The Saturday Evening Post* covers, all drawn by his owner, Al Staehle. Butch was so popular that he was immortalized with figurines, stuffed animals, a coloring book and even jigsaw puzzles.

Butch and his owner, artist Al Staehle are shown here on a visit to the offices of *The Saturday Evening Post*, surrounded by female admirers.

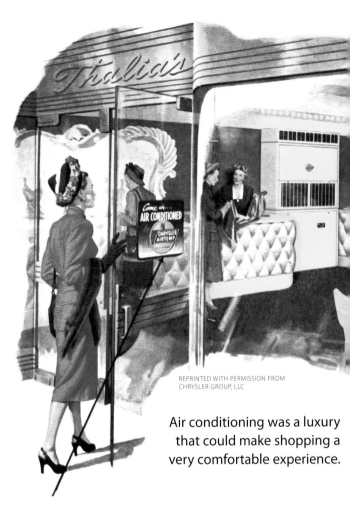

Air conditioning was a luxury that could make shopping a very comfortable experience.

Even with all the new products and innovations available, antiques could still stop customers in their tracks, causing them to reminisce.

Supermarkets, as opposed to small "Mom and Pop" stores, were becoming more and more popular after World War II.

Everyday Life

Where we shopped

Most Americans still shopped at locally owned shops for their clothing and apparel, but supermarkets and department stores were becoming more popular. Many small towns had "5 & 10" stores, like Woolworth's or Ben Franklin, where people could buy a variety of merchandise, and many towns still had general stores. Clerks were readily available, helping customers choose their purchases and wrapping them free of charge to take home.

Shoe stores featured full service, with clerks to measure your feet and fit your shoes. Clothing stores in cities offered a much larger selection of expensive goods, while rural shoppers either had to go to a dry goods store or choose clothing from a mail-order catalog.

Everyday Life

Service at its best

Lending a helping hand or providing professional surface often created a sense of bonding and friendship. Neighbors gladly helped each other change tires, lift heavy items or create solutions for everyday challenges. In return, they would often trade vegetables or enjoy inviting each other for a good home-cooked meal.

At the local corner meat market, service often came with a smile and local updates of interest. The neighborhood barber shop or beauty salon often provided answers to local questions. Receiving a haircut was only a small part of the total experience of learning the latest about neighborhood gossip.

Professional service often offered much more than what was called for. A visit to the gas station not only involved pumping gas. The one serving customers often cleaned the car windows, checked all of the fluids and tires and sometimes sent a treat home for the children and family.

1947 SWIFT & CO.

Quite often neighborhood professionals knew what their customers wanted before they even placed their order.

Law enforcement officers provided service to the elderly, children and those with special needs. Their knowledge of people in the neighborhood assisted in their personal reach to those on their beat.

asks such as changing tires or minor car repairs were often performed
vith a friendly visit to the customer.

Cutting hair was only a small part of a visit to the
barbershop. Those waiting would often exchange
ideas, give updates on the latest neighborhood
news and enjoy hearing the latest jokes.

A visit to the gas station included a full-service
checkup of fluids, cleaning the windshield and
monitoring tires.

The Metro Daily News

THE WEATHER
City and State—Rain,
Snow, Colder

FINAL
EDITION

10 PAGES   FIVE CENTS

VOLUME III—No. 184

SEPTEMBER 30, 1947

PAKISTAN AND YEMEN JOIN
THE UNITED NATIONS

Taking a break under a shade tree on a hot summer afternoon provided some time for friends to reflect on memories of farming days gone by.

The knowledge of the elderly in assisting with certain farming tasks was also a welcome gift to farm living.

Country Living

On the farm

Country living on the farm was a combination of earning money and carrying out self-sufficiency to meet the family needs. During the war, when there had been various food rationings, farm families survived well with their gardens and knowledge of processing foods. That tradition continued after the war as a means of saving money and providing healthy eating for family members.

Grandparents often lived with their children and grandchildren, providing a source of labor and an example of wise decision making to the younger generation. Country living meant teamwork. Children were each assigned chores ranging from weeding the garden to assisting with harvest and feeding farm animals.

Of course, there was always time for a neighborhood farm cookout on Sunday after church, singing around a campfire or playing the harmonica in the evening.

Tending a herd of livestock often took strategic planning and teamwork between farm workers.

Keeping track of animals was an important job for ranchers whose livestock spread out over large areas of land.

Country Living

On the ranch

Ranch living was much different than living on the family farm due to the larger expanses of land that owners were responsible for. Tending to large herds of cattle required teams of workers and sometimes, during times of crisis, staying all night on the range with the cattle.

Some ranches utilized the services of airplanes and high-tech tracking devices to keep an awareness of cattle locations or other ranch activity. Total family commitment was needed with each family member filling the respective role, whether it involved riding the range or staying back and preparing food and carrying out domestic responsibilities.

© 1947 SEPS

The Metro Daily News

FINAL EDITION

THE WEATHER
City all Store-Mart
Snow, Colder

VOLUME 87 — No. 161

70 PAGES   FIVE CENTS

OCTOBER 27, 1947

YOU BET YOUR LIFE WITH GROUCHO MARX, PREMIERES ON ABC RADIO IN THE U.S.

JOHN FALTER

Utilizing the services of small planes assisted in keeping track of livestock and other important tasks such as dusting crops and transporting important goods from one destination to another.

MEAD
SCHAEFFER

Moving cattle required a large organized team in order to keep the livestock together and moving in the right direction.

Everyday Life

Little helpers

The idea of family members helping each other taught a spirit of cooperation and teamwork that lasted for a lifetime. Responsibilities such as carrying in wood, washing dishes and caring for pets proved to be effective ways of learning responsibility early in life.

Some cooperative work moments brought special rewards. Experiences such as baking birthday cakes or making Christmas gifts proved to be a mixture of fun and work. In many homes, reaching out to help others became a means of teaching children the importance of thinking of others. Praise for accomplishments was effective in creating self-esteem and building self-confidence.

REPRINTED WITH PERMISSION OF
UNITED STATES STEEL CORPORATION

Helping mother iron clothes gave children a sense of helping with household chores.

1947 PYREX

Making a birthday cake always provided a special bond between mother and daughter.

1947 PYREX

Doing chores together strengthened family ties. Brothers and sisters learned to work together by doing dishes after the evening meal.

Carrying in wood after school was an everyday chore during the winter months.

1947 TIDE WATER ASSOCIATED OIL CO.

Children learned a sense of responsibility through caring for the family pet.

1947 LYON CORPORATION

Sons learned about car repair by working with their fathers.

FAMOUS BIRTHDAYS
Kevin Kline, October 24 actor
Hillary Rodham Clinton, October 26 former First Lady of the United States

Public recitation of memorized poems and readings was a regular part of demonstrating learning skills.

1947 EVERSHARP

Students often spent several hours at home working on preparation for the next day's classes.

Everyday Life

School days

Emphasis in school life was still based on the traditional reading, writing and arithmetic. Recitation played a big part in reading and English classes. Poems such as, "The Midnight Ride of Paul Revere," and other history-related literature was memorized and quoted in front of the entire class. That meant lots of time working on preparation in the evening. Homework time was usually very interactive with parents helping children with memorizing, working out math problems and memorizing spelling words.

Discipline was strict; teachers didn't hesitate to use paddles or engage in such disciplines as asking students to stand in the corner or in the hallway outside the classroom door. Parents supported teachers' efforts to teach and correct their children. As a result, a general atmosphere of respect was expected for educators, who dressed formally to carry out their daily tasks.

Social activities such as festivals, spelling bees and programs were considered rewards for hard work.

Teachers were stern and demanding in drilling students in learning exercises.

"There's a certain young man who's delaying this movie for the rest of the class."

Those in rural areas were forced to bundle up in warm clothing to wait at the school bus stop.

Music Entertained Us

Most American households did not have a television in 1947, so radio and records were still a great source of entertainment. Radios and phonographs were becoming smaller and more affordable. People also enjoyed listening to coin-operated phonographs (later called jukeboxes) when they went out to restaurants and bars.

People still enjoyed playing music in the home, and lots of parents thought that music lessons (particularly piano) were an important part of a happy childhood.

1947 WURLITZER MUSIC COMPANY

In 1947, records were still 78 rpms. More and more homes had their own phonographs, making it easier for teenagers to listen to their favorite tunes.

"We dread the day when he gets big enough to use the loud pedal."

1947 STROMBERG-CARLSON CORPORATION

Teens were often in the band and choir at school, and they enjoyed getting together for some practice. Many homes had pianos (upright models were popular), and piano lessons were a rite of passage.

This more compact Philco radio/phonograph allowed you to slide the record in, close the door and have it play automatically, making it easier for the whole family to use.

norman rockwell

The Metro Daily News

FINAL EDITION

NOVEMBER 6, 1947

PROGRAM *MEET THE PRESS* MAKES ITS TELEVISION DEBUT ON THE NBC-TV NETWORK

© GETTY IMAGES

Vernon Cass and Pam Leslie demonstrate "The Astaire," the new fox-trot that Fred Astaire created. Swing dancing, fox-trots and Latin dances were quite popular.

REPRINTED WITH PERMISSION OF WELCH FOODS INC.

High school dances provided opportunities for slow dancing, and chaperones kept couples from dancing too close!

Very formal dances at colleges, clubs or ballrooms called for love gowns, tuxedo and dancing the traditional waltz.

1947 DECCA RECORDS

We Loved to Dance

In 1947, people loved to dance—at home, in the high school gym, at clubs, in ballrooms. The big band era was ending, and solo singers like Bing Crosby and Frank Sinatra topped the charts, but swing dancing was just as popular as ever, with lots of people doing the Lindy Hop. Ballroom style dances like the fox-trot and the waltz were still staples, and Latin dancing, like the mambo and the rumba, were making their way to mainstream America.

Famous for his extraordinary dances in films, Fred Astaire went on to cofound Fred Astaire Dance Studios in 1947. His studios, along with already established Arthur Murray Dance Studios and others, were great places for couples to learn everything from the rumba to the fox-trot.

Teenage girls always seemed willing to demonstrate the latest steps.

1947 SPARKS-WITHINGTON CO.

Clock radios were now available in plastic and in different colors too. They were also advertised as great table radios.

Radio/phonographs, with automatic record changers that could play up to 12 records automatically, were high on the public's wish list.

This Westinghouse Consolette featured a lift-out radio to move from room to room, plus a phonograph with automatic record changer and lots of storage space in the blond oak cabinet.

Entertainment on the Air

Television was just getting started, but it was not available in many parts of the country. Radio was still king, and with new, smaller models available, they were more affordable than ever before. Innovations like the radio/phonograph and the clock radio were popular, coveted items. Radios/ phonographs were also being incorporated into furniture pieces since they were an important part of the home.

This General Electric television ad stated that their TV's were being featured by dealers in "those cities where television programs are now available."

Radio/phonographs were being combined with furniture craftsmanship so they would blend in with living room decor.

Its Smart

Its Compact

Its Powerf

Top Hits of 1947

"Near You"
Francis Craig

"Heartaches"
Ted Weems

"Smoke! Smoke! Smoke! (That Cigarette)"
Tex Williams

"The Old Lamp-Lighter"
Sammy Kaye

"Almost Like Being In Love"
Jo Stafford

"Ballerina"
Vaughn Monroe

"Peg o' My Heart"
The Harmonicats

"Chi-Baba, Chi-Baba (My Bambino Go to Sleep)"
Perry Como

"Managua, Nicaragua"
Freddy Martin

"Mam'selle"
Art Lund

"(I Love You) For Sentimental Reasons"
The King Cole Trio

"Open the Door, Richard"
Count Basie

"Zip-a-Dee-Doo-Dah"
James Basket

Entertainment on the Air

Top hits

With television in its infancy, radio was still where most people turned for entertainment. One could enjoy everything from *The Adventures of Sam Spade* or the *Lone Ranger* to *Fibber McGee & Molly* or Edgar Bergen & Charlie McCarthy.

Solo singers like Jo Stafford, Perry Como and Ted Weems had more top hits than the big bands, but the famous big band leader, Sammy Kaye, did score a top hit in 1947.

Jo Stafford had a big hit with "Almost Like Being in Love."

famous big band leader Sammy Kaye (seen here with vocalists Tony Alamo and Laura Leslie) had a big hit with "The Old Lamp-Lighter."

Radio Stars & Hits of 1947

Adventures of Ellery Queen

Adventures of Sam Spade

Amos 'n' Andy

Bing Crosby

Captain Midnight

Crime Club

Edgar Bergen & Charlie McCarthy

Escape

The Falcon

Fibber McGee & Molly

The Lone Ranger

Sherlock Homes

This is Your FBI

Edgar Bergen (left), the ventriloquist, and his stage dummy Charlie McCarthy were one of the most successful comedy teams on the radio in 1947.

The Argus Argoflex camera featured a view finder to show the picture before capturing the moment.

1947 ARGUS INC.

REPRINTED WITH PERMISSION FROM 3M

LOOK FOR THIS TAG WHEN YOU BUY SPORTSWEAR

FABRIC TREATED WITH
Du Pont
ZELAN
DURABLE
REPELLENT FINISH
Approved for repellency by
BETTER FABRICS TESTING BUREAU, Inc.

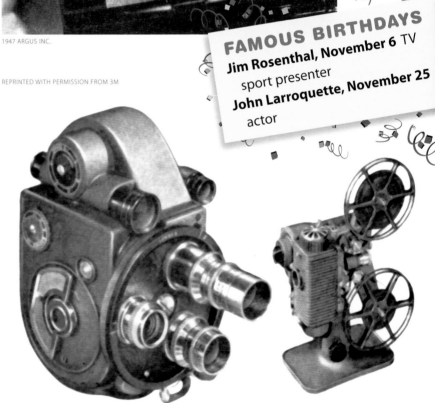

The Revere-Eight movie camera by Revere Camera Company made taking home movies surprisingly easy.

Moments Captured

Cameras and movie makers

Major improvements in the ability to focus cameras more accurately encouraged greater participation in everyday family picture taking. In 1947, The Argus 35mm Markfinder camera included guidelines to help capture picture subjects more accurately. The Argoflex model camera advertised a viewfinder which made it easy to frame and focus pictures.

Movie cameras were being simplified to make it easier to capture everyday moments of life. Cameras became more popular as a gift-giving item, especially for special occasions such as Father's Day and Christmas. Viewing home movies became a social event in which the entire family gathered together for a night of watching movies and eating snacks. Making photograph albums became a popular way of tucking away special memories and keepsakes for future generations to view.

Revere Eight Magazine movie camera

Filmo Auto Load movie camera by Bell & Howell Co.

The Argus Model 21 camera with the amazing Markfinder

At the Movies

1947 brought us some enduring favorites, especially two holiday films we still watch today: *The Bishop's Wife* and *Miracle on 34th Street*. Light comedies were popular with audiences—films like *The Bachelor and the Bobby-Soxer*, *The Egg and I* and *Road to Rio*.

Drama and passion won the day with the movie *Unconquered*, tops at the box office. *Forever Amber*, dishing up too much romance for some people's taste, was based on the controversial bestselling book, *Forever Amber*, which upset moralists.

Left to right: John Payne, Maureen O-Hara, Edmund Gwenn (dressed as Santa, he won the Academy Award for Best Supporting Actor for the role) and young Natalie Wood gaze at a Christmas tree in director George Seaton's film *Miracle on 34th Street*. The film is still a holiday staple for families.

DARRYL F. ZANUCK *presents*

GREGORY PECK
DOROTHY McGUIRE
JOHN GARFIELD

in

Laura Z. Hobson's

Gentleman's Agreement

Celeste Anne June Albert Jane Dean
HOLM · REVERE · HAVOC · DEKKER · WYATT · STOCKWELL

PRODUCED BY ARRYL F. ZANUCK · SCREEN PLAY BY MOSS HART · DIRECTED BY ELIA KAZAN

20th CENTURY-FOX TRIUMPH!

Gentleman's Agreement, directed by Elia Kazan, and starring Gregory Peck, Dorothy McGuire and John Garfield won the Academy Award for Best Picture.

The Metro Daily News

FINAL EDITION

DECEMBER 3, 1947

THE TENNESSEE WILLIAMS PLAY A STREETCAR NAMED DESIRE OPENS ON BROADWAY

Unconquered, directed by Cecil B. DeMille, was the top-grossing film of 1947. Starring Paulette Goddard and Gary Cooper, one of the film's taglines was, "I bought this woman for my own and I'll kill the man who touches her!"

Cary Grant, Shirley Temple and Myrna Loy are seen here in a publicity shot for *The Bachelor and the Bobby-Soxer*. The film tied with *The Egg and I* as the second highest grossing picture of the year.

Tops at the Box Office

We were having lunch the other day with an artist friend, and happened to remark that we had never been to Hollywood and wondered what it looked like. "I've never been to Hollywood, either," he said, "but it prob-ably looks like this." And handing us the check to hold, he made the sketch which is reproduced above. Personally, we think the guy has been to Hollywood.

At the Movies

The stars

The films of 1947 starred or were directed by some of Hollywood's most enduring legends. Cecil B. DeMille, who directed the 1947 hit, *Unconquered*, is also famous for *The Ten Commandments* and *The King of Kings*. Producer Darryl Zanuck, also known for his films like *The Grapes of Wrath* and *All About Eve*, brought us the best film of 1947, *Gentlemen's Agreement*.

Already famous stars like Gary Cooper, William Powell, Irene Dunne and Myrna Loy lit up the screen, while newcomers like Janet Leigh and Marilyn Monroe made their film debut in 1947.

© 1947 SEPS

1. Gary Cooper, 2. Ingrid Bergman, 3. Melvyn Douglas, 4. Ginger Rogers, 5. Marlene Dietrich, 6. Bob Hope, 7. Greer Garson, 8. Bette Davis, 9. Bing Crosby, 10. Jean Gabin, 11. Ronald Colman, 12. James Cagney, 13. Victor Mature,.14. Red Skelton, 15. W. C. Fields, 16. Dorothy Lamour, 17. Adolphe Menjou, 18. Charles Boyer, 19. Edward G. Robinson, 20. Rosalind Russell, 21. Spencer Tracy, 22. Clark Gable, 23. Charles Laughton, 24. Katharine Hepburn, 25. Mickey Rooney, 26. William Powell, 27. Veronica Lake, 28. Monty Woolley, 29. Margaret O'Brien, 30. Cary Grant, 31. Claudette Colbert, 32. Joan Bennett, 33. Van Johnson, 34-35. Abbott and Costello, 36. Sonja Henie, 37. Gregory Peck, 38. Fred Astaire, 39. Johnny Weissmuller, 40. Groucho Marx, 41. Harpo Marx, 42. Carmen Miranda.

Y IMAGES

1947 Oscar winners at the Academy Awards—Left to right: Best Producer Darryl Zanuck (*Gentlemen's Agreement*), Best Actress Loretta Young (*The Farmer's Daughter*), Best Supporting Actor Edmund Gwenn (*Miracle on 34th Street*); Best Supporting Actress Celeste Holm (*Gentlemen's Agreement*) and Best Actor Ronald Colman (*A Double Life*).

Winter Fun

For those raised in areas of heavy snowfall, the desire to continue doing outside activities brought about numerous creative ways of having winter fun. In many cases, items laying around the property became useful as winter toys. Tires, feed sacks and homemade sleds left their marks of family memories on snow-covered hillsides.

In many neighborhoods, a competitive spirit grew in the creation of snowmen, snow forts and other winter sculptures. Those gathering to ice skate on farm ponds often enjoyed treats such as homemade donuts, cookies or hot chocolate. In other cases, crackling bonfires warmed the hearts of those enjoying outside activities.

© 1947 SEPS

"It's simple mathematics, for heaven's sake. You're paying him 30 cents an hour and, after all, a new windshield wiper only costs $1.50!"

© 1947 SEPS

A set of ice skates tossed over a shoulder of an excited youngster meant an afternoon of fun at the local frozen pond.

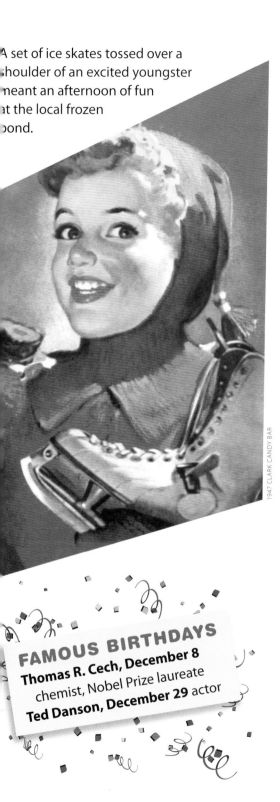

The neighborhood gang enjoyed an afternoon of tobogganing on the slopes of country hillsides.

FAMOUS BIRTHDAYS
Thomas R. Cech, December 8
chemist, Nobel Prize laureate
Ted Danson, December 29 actor

All I Want for Christmas

Steel production had turned to consumer goods, so everyone, from Mom and Dad to the kids, had lots of innovative appliances, electronics and toys from which to choose. Busy moms were happy to get the latest appliance, like a two tub Easy washing machine.

Parents could save live memories of their children with devices like the Recordio recording radio-phonograph.

Kids wanted new bikes, wagons and doll carriages, things made from steel that hadn't been available during the war years. Popular items were dolls and doll houses for girls and train sets for boys.

REPRINTED WITH PERMISSION OF UNITED STATES STEEL CORPORATION

New trikes and doll carriages made of steel were once again for sale, keeping Santa quite busy with kids' long Christmas lists!

WASHES A FULL LOAD HERE

EASY *Spin Rinser*

RINSES AND DAMP DRIES HERE

With the help of advertisers, kids knew exactly what they wanted for Christmas, and you can be sure that lots of boys and girls put a shiny, brand new bike at the top of their list.

What Made Us Laugh

"I've heard a lot about you."

"Don't you have something that isn't so confounded merry and jolly?"

While in Chicago, artist Norman Rockwell set up props in the Marshall Field department store with all kinds of toys for this Dec. 27, 1947 *Post* cover. His biggest trouble was shopping for a salesgirl. After looking for several weeks, Rockwell found a waitress in a tavern who had just the look he was searching for.

More *The Saturday Evening Post* Covers

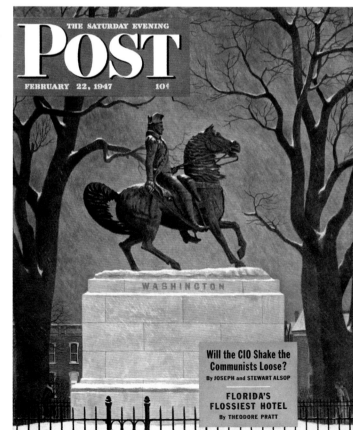

The Saturday Evening Post covers were works of art, many illustrated by famous artists of the time, including Norman Rockwell. Most of the 1947 covers have been incorporated within the previous pages of this book; the few that were not are presented on the following pages for your enjoyment.

MORE FAMOUS BIRTHDAYS

January 8
Dave Smyth, musician/record producer
Laurie Walters, actress

January 9
Ronnie Landfield, artist

January 16
Laura Schlessinger, psychologist and radio talk show host

January 16
Apasra Hongsakula, Miss Universe 1965

January 24
Michio Kaku, theoretical physicist

January 24
Masashi Ozaki, Japanese golfer

January 29
Linda B. Buck, biologist

January 31
Nolan Ryan, baseball player

February 1
Jessica Savitch, journalist

February 2
Farrah Fawcett, actress

February 3
Paul Auster, novelist

February 4
Dennis C. Blair, admiral

February 5
Darrell Waltrip, race car driver and broadcaster

February 7
Wayne Allwine, voice actor

February 15
John Coolidge Adams, composer

February 18
Princess Christina, Netherlands
Dennis DeYoung, rock musician

February 24
Edward James Olmos, actor

February 25
Doug Yule, rock singer and musician

February 26
Sandie Shaw, British singer

March 1
Alan Thicke, actor

March 4
David Franzoni, screenwriter

March 6
Dick Fosbury, athlete

March 10
Tom Scholz, musician, songwriter and inventor

March 12
Mitt Romney, former Governor of Massachusetts

March 15
Ry Cooder, guitarist

March 19
Glenn Close, actress

March 24
Alan Sugar, English entrepreneur

March 27
Walt Mossberg, newspaper columnist

April 2
Emmylou Harris, singer
Camille Paglia, literary critic

April 8
Tom DeLay, politician

April 12
Tom Clancy, author
David Letterman, talk show host

April 15
Lois Chiles, actress

April 18
James Woods, actor

April 19
Murray Perahia, pianist

April 21
Iggy Pop, rock musician

April 28
Ken St. Andre, game designer and author

April 30
Leslie Grantham, British actor

May 4
Theda Skocpol, sociologist

May 8
H. Robert Horvitz, biologist, recipient of Nobel Prize in Physiology or Medicine

May 12
Michael Ignatieff, Canadian public intellectual, philosopher and historian

May 19
Paul Brady, Northern Irish singer/songwriter

May 27
Peter DeFazio, politician

June 1
Ronnie Wood, English rock musician

June 6
Robert Englund, actor

June 7
Thurman Munson, baseball catcher

June 8
Eric F. Wieschaus, biologist, recipient of Nobel Prize in Physiology of Medicine

June 14
Barry Melton, rock musician

June 20
Candy Clark, actress

June 22
Octavia E. Butler, author
David Lander, actor and baseball scout
Pete Maravich, basketball player

June 25
Jimmie Walker, actor

June 28
Mark Helprin, writer

July 2
Larry David, actor, writer, producer and director

July 3
Betty Buckley, actress

July 6
Barnelle Harris, musician

July 8
Bobby Sowell, pianist and composer

July 9
Mitch Mitchell, English rock drummer

July 19
Brian May, English rock guitarist

July 20
Gerd Binnig, German physicist, Nobel Prize laureate
Carlos Santana, Mexican-born rock guitarist

July 22
Albert Brooks, actor
Don Henley, singer/songwriter and musician

July 23
Spencer Christian, television weather reporter

July 24
Peter Serkin, pianist

August 9
John Varley, science-fiction author

August 10
Ian Anderson, British rock musician

August 12
William Hartston, British chess player

August 14
Maddy Prior, English folk singer

August 19
Gerard Schwarz, conductor

August 27
Barbara Bach, actress

August 28
Liza Wang, Hong Kong actress

August 29
Temple Grandin, animal welfare and autism expert

August 31
Ramon Castellano de Torres, Spanish painter

September 1
Al Green, politician

September 6
Jane Curtin, actress and comedian

September 14
Sam Neill, New Zealand actor

September 30
Marc Bolan, English rock musician
Rula Lenska, British actress

October 1
Aaron Ciechanover, Israeli biologist, recipient of Nobel Prize in Chemistry

October 6
Gail Farrell, singer

October 13
Sammy Hagar, rock singer

October 16
Bob Weir, rock guitarist

October 17
Gene Green, politician
Michael McKean, actor and comedian

October 26
Jaclyn Smith, actress

October 29
Richard Dreyfuss, actor

November 8
Minnie Riperton, R&B singer

November 10
Glen Buxton, rock guitarist

November 14
P.J. O'Rourke, journalist and satirist

November 15
Steven G. Kellman, author and critic

November 19
Bob Boone, baseball player and manager

November 20
Joe Walsh, rock singer, songwriter and guitarist

November 23
Diana Quick, actress

November 24
Mike Gorman, sports announcer

November 30
David Mamet, playwright

December 7
Wendy Padbury, British actress

December 9
Tom Daschle, politician

December 14
Christopher Parkening, guitarist

December 16
Vincent Matthews, athlete

December 21
Paco de Lucía, Spanish guitarist

December 26
Carlton Fisk, baseball player

December 31
Burton Cummings, Canadian rock musician
Tim Matheson, actor

Facts and Figures of 1947

President of the U.S.
Harry S. Truman
Vice President of the U.S.
Alben W. Barkley

Population of the U.S.
144,126,071

Births
3,817,000

College Graduates
Males: 175,615
Females: 95,571

Average Salary for full-time employee: $2,603.00
Minimum Wage (per hour): $0.40

HARRY S. TRUMAN LIBRARY

Average cost for:

Bread (lb.)...............................$0.13

Bacon (lb.)..............................$0.78

Butter (lb.)..............................$0.81

Eggs (doz.)..............................$0.70

Milk (gal.)................................$0.78

Potatoes (10 lbs.)..................$0.50

Coffee (lb.)..............................$0.47

Sugar (5 lb.)............................$0.49

Gasoline (gal.).........................$0.15

Movie Ticket...........................$0.35

Postage Stamp.......................$0.03

Car.....................................$1,300.00

Single-Family home... $6,600.00

1947 SWIFT & CO.

REPRINTED WITH PERMISSION FROM FORD MOTOR COMPANY

Notable Inventions and Firsts

January 23: Duke Ellington plays at New York City's Carnegie Hall for the first time.

February 17: The *Voice of America* begins to transmit radio broadcasts to Eastern Europe and the Soviet Union.

February 21: In New York City, Edwin Land demonstrates the first "instant" camera", his Polaroid Land Camera, to a meeting of the Optical Society of America.

May 22: In an effort to fight the spread of Communism, President Harry S. Truman signs an Act of Congress that implements the Truman Doctrine. This Act grants $400 million in military and economic aid to Turkey and Greece.

© GETTY IMAGES

May 22: David Lean's film *Great Expectations,* based on the novel by Charles Dickens, opens in the U.S. Critics call it the finest film ever made from a Charles Dickens novel.

July 11: The ship *Exodus* leaves France for Palestine with 4,500 Jewish Holocaust survivor refugees on board. One week later on July 18 the ship is captured by British troops and refused entry into Palestine at the port of Haifa.

October 20: Radio rights for the World Series sell for $475,000 for three years.

November 2: In California, the designer and airplane pilot Howard Hughes performs the maiden flight of the *Spruce Goose,* the largest fixed-wing aircraft ever built. The flight lasts only eight minutes and the *Spruce Goose* is never flown again.

Sports Winners

NFL: Chicago Cardinals defeat Philadelphia Eagles
World Series: New York Yankees defeat Brooklyn Dodgers
Stanley Cup: Toronto Maple Leafs defeat Montreal Canadiens
The Masters: Jimmy Demaret wins
PGA Championship: Jim Ferrier wins

REPRINTED WITH PERMISSION OF CHEVRON AND EXXON MOBIL COMPANIES

Live It Again 1947

PROJECT EDITOR	Barb Sprunger
ART DIRECTOR	Brad Snow
COPYWRITERS	Jill Case, Jim Langham
COPY SUPERVISOR	Deborah Morgan
EDITORIAL ASSISTANT	Stephanie Smith
PRODUCTION ARTIST SUPERVISOR	Erin Augsburger
PRODUCTION ARTIST	Erin Augsburger
COPY EDITOR	Amanda Scheerer
PHOTOGRAPHY SUPERVISOR	Tammy Christian
NOSTALGIA EDITOR	Ken Tate
EDITORIAL DIRECTOR	Jeanne Stauffer
PUBLISHING SERVICES DIRECTOR	Brenda Gallmeyer

Printed in China
First Printing: 2011
Library of Congress Number: 2010904349
ISBN: 978-1-59217-306-8

Customer Service
LiveItAgain.com
(800) 829-5865

1 2 3 4 5 6 7 8 9